After the Affair

Emotional Healing God's Way

Arnita L. Fields

Unity Three Publications
Memphis, Tennessee

Introduction

When God commissioned me to write this book, I was instructed to share with readers like you the life-changing tools which were given to me by my heavenly father as I walked through the emotional healing process after a series of affairs which almost destroyed my marriage. For the next few moments, we will look at the term *"adultery"* to gain an understanding as to what it is as well as look at what the word of God says concerning it.

By looking at the meaning of the word *"adultery"*, we will see that it is described in Merriam Webster Dictionary as *"voluntary sexual intercourse between a married man and someone other than his wife or between a married woman and someone other than her husband."*

To gain an even greater understanding of what the word means, we find that there is an additional term which has gained greater exposure in recent years. The term *"Emotional Adultery"* is described as *an affair which excludes physical intimacy but includes emotional intimacy with someone or something other than his or her spouse, which causes a breech in the covenant relationship.* Although not relegated to someone of the opposite sex, *"emotional adultery"* can also be seen in areas such business or job, co-workers, chat lines or groups, drug or food addictions, Internet sex, pornography, family or friends.

The Multi-Version Bible Concordance reveals that the word **adultery** occurs 49 different times in the Bible, including in the book of Revelation. In addition to being seen as a social issue, it is of course seen as a sin in the eyes of the Father. In the word of God – from Genesis to

Revelation – you will find a variety of verses which speak on the subject of adultery.

The verses God has included in the Bible are there to help shed light on what a spouse can do when faced with adultery within their own marriage.

Matthew 19:9 gives a very specific answer for those who desire to move forth. It reads, *"I tell you that anyone who divorces his wife, except for sexual immorality, and marries another woman commits adultery."* When faced with the decision whether or not to divorce after an affair, a spouse using prayer in addition to the word of God as their guide has a better opportunity to make a decision based on God's divine purpose for their marriage.

There are several questions that remain to be asked and answered: 1) What do you do if while reading this book you realize that your spouse has been committing emotional adultery? 2) Should you call up your family, friends and in-laws or run down to the nearest divorce attorney? 3) How would you respond if God reveals that He desires for you to remain in your marriage? 4) Would you submit to follow His plans or would you run to the hills? 5) How do you move past the pain and hurt you have experienced if both you and your spouse desire to make your marriage work?

Know that an act of emotional or physical adultery should not result in the end your marriage. If you have recently experienced or are still recovering from the after effects of your spouse's emotional or physical affair (s), *After the Affair: Emotionally Healing God's Way* is a book which contains practical tools that will help show you how to move forward in your divine purpose in a healthy and Godly manner. May you be encouraged, find hope and comfort, as well as be strengthened in your inner man with what the Father has released to be shared in this book.

Blessings & Love,

Arnita L. Fields
Christian Counselor

Acknowledgements

Heavenly Father, you have continued to amaze me with your ways. You are totally incredible. Thank you for keeping me centered in your Holy truth and divine will.

To Anthony, my husband of 15 years: Father has shown us through the years that our love for each other is truly real. Thank you for sharing this covenant marriage journey with me. There's no other place I'd rather be.

For every husband and wife who placed their faith in the Father's hands: May Father God bless you richly for your obedience and willingness in allowing Him to teach you how to forgive, release, love, trust and to respect your covenant spouse again.

Thank you so much Prophetess Renee for your encouragement and dedicated intercession concerning this scribal assignment. God said it and it has surely come to pass.

Thanks so much to Dr. Zipporah Brown, the facilitators and intercessors of Paga Global Prayer Connections (PAGA), who have prayed earnestly this past year concerning the scribal assignments God has ordained for me to complete. Your prayers and labor of love will not be forgotten.

Table of Contents

Welcome to the Beginning
of Your Emotional Healing

If you are looking for an outlet to help encourage negativity towards your spouse following an act of emotional or physical infidelity, then this book is not for you. However, if you are looking for hope, this self-help guide is filled with practical wisdom along with prayers, my personal testimonial nuggets and the word of God to help you refocus on what's important.

This book is written to help instruct and encourage people who have experienced emotional or physical infidelity within their marriages. The simple steps shared inside these pages will help to guide individuals, couples or participants in a small support group back onto the right path and to receive and experience the emotional healing which God has freely made available for them.

It's Okay to Grieve –
But, Don't Dwell There (Poem)

It's okay to grieve once you face reality – the reality of betrayal within your home.

The loss of trust and intimacy with your covenant spouse has led to your sudden grief.

Don't dig in your heels. There's no time to live in defeat. It's time to get up and to shake yourself. It's time to be loosed from your grief.

The pain, shame, bitterness and anger should be kicked to the curb. There's no time to stand still and let grief maintain a foothold in the corridors of your soul.

Never allow any misplaced blame to ride free upon your back. Pack up all of its bags, and then escort this uninvited guest right up out of your house.

Today is a brand new day for God's truth to come your way. It's time to get your spirit and your mind back on track.

Keep your heart with all diligence, for out of it spring the issues of life. Put away from you a deceitful mouth, and put perverse lips far from you. Let your eyes look straight ahead, and your eyelids look right before you. Ponder the path of your feet, and let all your ways be established. Do not turn to the right or the left; remove your foot from evil.

Step One: Assessing Your Wounds (Heart)

Father, create in me a clean heart and purify me.

After the initial discovery of your spouse's affair, you may find yourself going through a range of emotions. While it is normal to experience anger, disgust, bitterness, hatred, or even feelings of betrayal, at the end of the day, it's the manner in how you process and release your emotions that's really important. After you have released the toxic emotions, what happens next? What is the right way to deal with the hurt, pain and betrayal that has surfaced as a result of your spouse's affair? In this chapter, you will be given tools to help you learn how to assess your wounds in a healthy manner.

First, we will look at the different stages of grief and why it is not only normal but a necessary process that people should go through when faced with any type of loss.

1. **Denial** – In the first step, there is an initial shock that one feels immediately upon hearing about a loss. Experiencing a loss is not just limited to a death but can include relationships, job, finances or possessions.

2. **<u>Anger</u>** – Occurs once reality of the loss begins to set in. This is where the person experiencing the loss looks for someone to blame for their loss.

3. **<u>Bargaining</u>** – Happens when the person facing the loss begins to bargain with God in an attempt to have returned what was lost.

4. **<u>Depression</u>** – May contain additional feelings of anger and guilt. With this step, the person facing the loss seeks to blame themselves for the loss they are now facing.

5. **<u>Acceptance</u>** – Is the final step in the grieving process. This is where the hurt associated with the loss is accepted and deep reflection of the memories shared with those they have lost begins.

The grief process is not limited to a certain timetable and can last anywhere from a few months up until three years, depending on the individual and the type of loss experienced. If a person experiences deep and sorrowful grief, it is essential and beneficial for them to seek out the help of a grief counselor or a mental health care professional.

Now that we have got an understanding concerning the basic concept of the grief process, we will move on to discuss how you can assess your wounds. In order to check where your wounds begin, you would need to look at the central area next to the brain in the human body –and, that's the heart. Taking time out to look within is important and takes courage to open your heart so it can be cleansed of any impurities.

There are several steps that must take place in order to fully assess your wounds:

1. Be honest and open with yourself about how you are feeling.

It is okay and absolutely normal for you to reveal that you are hurt and you are experiencing anger after learning of your spouse's affair. Now is the time to freely face the fear of hiding behind a mask like nothing has happened. If you can do so with the help of a close friend or confidant, allow for your emotions to release from the buildup of steam in a healthy manner. If you have a need to scream or cry, go ahead and do so. Allow some time for your healing to come forth by releasing and not allowing your emotions to stay bottled up. When your emotions can't release in a healthy manner, bitterness has an opportunity to take root and cause a delay in the healing process.

2. Be honest and open with God as you seek Him for understanding.

If you have a consistent relationship with God, you know that He is available to talk with you at anytime. Spend some time in worship and praise before Him. By focusing on the attributes of the Heavenly Father, it will lead you into a place of peace. It does not mean that you are not hurting but it does allow for you to rest and regain strength in the presence of God. When you have the peace of God in your life, you can hear clearly. When you hear clearly, you are able to make godly and wise decisions.

3. Be honest and open with your spouse as you discuss the root cause of the affair.

If you have the opportunity to speak with your spouse upon discovery or after learning of their affair, speak with them in a normal conversational mode. Pray before speaking. Never allow your emotions to lead and guide you where you don't want to go. Remember you still represent Christ. Once you open up to your spouse and release all that God allows you to share, then give your spouse the opportunity to talk. If your spouse is being evasive and not willing to share or discuss the details of their affair, don't press or argue with them to get answers. Pull back, pray and wait on God to show you how to strategically move concerning the issue. Allow God the opportunity to orchestrate what happens next.

As we prepare to move on to the next step in healing God's way, you will now have an opportunity to spend some time answering questions for self reflection. Once you have answered the questions, take some time to pause and pray before proceeding to the next chapter. If you feel at this time that you will need the assistance of a professional counselor or mental health care professional, check with your local church, clinic or hospital for more information.

Personal Testimony Nugget

When I first learned of my husband's affair, it was through a dream. Surprised and relieved all at the same time, I knew that what God was allowing me to see during this time was His way of not allowing me to find out through the "in-law grapevine" so to speak.

After a time of prayer and talking with a friend who was my prayer mentor at that time, I knew I was at peace about the next step of going to my husband with what I knew. Of course, he was surprised that I even knew anything about what was going on, but none the less, the covers had been pulled back on how he had officially defiled our marriage bed. With the ball now officially in his court, I came home from work one evening to a "Dear Nita" letter. Despite my husband's response to what was going on in our marriage, God had called me to a greater place of accountability in my walk with Him and I had to do things His way.

Did I always do everything as instructed during our separation? No not at all. But, I knew that I had to find my place in God's presence and remain there so He could heal my broken heart and begin the work that was so desperately needed in my marriage.

Step One: Questions for Self-Reflection

1.   Have you personally acknowledged to God your feelings about your spouse's affair?

2.   What steps have you taken to seek help for yourself?

3.   What is the hardest thing up to this point that you had to deal with in your marriage? Explain

4.   How were you able to move past the difficulties? Explain

5.   Are you dealing with any residue of hurt/pain from previous relationships? Explain

6.   What are some of the things you would like for God to do in your own life?

7.   What are some of the things you would like for God to do in your marriage?

8.   Are you willing to submit to and walk through the healing process God's way?

9.   Are you willing to commit to a time of prayer and consecration to hear from God concerning your life?

Mark 11:25
And whenever you stand praying, if you have anything against anyone, forgive him that your Father in heaven may also forgive you your trespasses.

Step Two: Walking in True Forgiveness (Spirit)

"I choose to forgive, I choose to release"

"I release the hurt, the betrayal and the shame. I release you from breaking my heart and causing me so much pain. I choose to forgive. I choose to release despite how you made me feel. And, because My Father the Sovereign God has been way too good to me, I'm free and so are you. I release you my dear spouse as Jesus my Savior and Lord has taught me to do. I choose to forgive. I choose to release, not only for you but most importantly for me."

After assessing your wounds and allowing your heart to be cleansed, the next area that will be addressed is that of forgiveness. Walking by faith in true forgiveness is essential not just in your covenant marriage relationship, but in all of your relationships. So how can you walk in forgiveness with a spouse who has betrayed you?

Despite what may be going though your mind right now concerning the proceeding question, walking in forgiveness is not really as hard as it is often made out to be. First let's take a moment to look at the definition of the word.

Forgiveness is described as: **The act of forgiving; or to pardon**.

In order to walk in forgiveness, you will have to perform

the act of actually releasing your spouse from any unforgiveness that you have towards them. Now, let's go to the word of God to see how walking in forgiveness is more important than anything that has happened in your marriage.

John 8: 3-11 says:

3 Then the scribes and Pharisees brought to Him a woman caught in adultery. And when they had sat her in the midst,

4 They said to him, Teacher, this woman was caught in adultery, in the very act.

5 Now Moses in the law commanded us, that such should be stoned: but what do you say?

6 This they said, testing him, that they might have something of which to accuse him. But Jesus stooped down, and wrote on the ground with his finger, as though he did not hear.

7 So when they continued asking him, he raised himself up and said to them, **He who is without sin among you, let him throw a stone at her first**.

8 And again he stooped down and wrote on the ground.

9 Then those who heard it, being convicted by their conscience, went out one by one, beginning with the oldest even to the last. And Jesus was left alone, and the woman standing in the midst.

10 When Jesus had raised himself up and saw no one but the woman, he said to her, **Woman, where are those**

accusers of yours? Has no one condemned you?

11 She said, No one Lord. And Jesus said to her, **Neither do I condemn you; go and sin no more.**

In viewing the verses in John 8:3-11, we see that the woman caught in adultery is brought to Jesus by her accusers. What was meant to end her life would eventually be the start of a new life for her. According to the letter of the law, she was to be stoned to death for her act of adultery, but because of the forgiveness of her sins by Jesus, she had an opportunity to leave her past behind and walk free of condemnation from her accusers.

Jesus made it clear in verse 7 that if there was anyone without sin in their lives, they were welcome to throw the first stone at the woman. When they each began to reflect on their individual lives and the fact that they each had areas of sin in their own lives, they each walked off and left the woman alone with Jesus.

In your own life, how many times have you failed God and committed sins, only to be forgiven? When others accused and sometimes caught you in the very act, how did you respond? If you can accept and receive forgiveness from God, it is essential that you also extend forgiveness as well.

Does extending forgiveness to your spouse for committing adultery take them off the hook? No, but it does give them an opportunity to be alone with Jesus to answer to the sin of adultery. When you change your perspective and began to look inward at the status of your own heart, you will begin to learn how to walk in compassion with those who have fallen short in their walk with Christ. While forgiveness is a requirement of God for everyone, its purpose or goal is not to decrease the fact that you may still be hurt concerning the pain your spouse has caused in your marriage.

At the end of the day, you hold the key to not only your own healing but the healing of your spouse as well. So, what happens next after you have embraced and put into action the forgiveness process? For starters, if you keep these four keys in mind, you will have no problem walking in forgiveness with anyone. Know that:

1. God requires us to walk in forgiveness.

2. The pathway to your healing begins with forgiveness.

3. When we don't forgive others, we condemn them.

4. Forgiveness leads to a greater intimacy with God and your spouse.

As we come to the close of this chapter, it is important to remember that walking in true forgiveness takes an individual act of humility and obedience to God. Your opinion on how you feel about your spouse's affair or any other sins your spouse has committed should not dictate how or when you should forgive. Walking in true forgiveness is not an option but a requirement in order for you to stay in right relationship with God.

As you reflect on what you learned concerning forgiveness, take a few moments to pray before answering the self-refection questions for this chapter. Your response and what your heart reveals will determine the area of greatest need to work on. If you need an accountability partner to walk though this process with you, select someone who is not afraid of being open and honest with you.

Personal Testimony Nugget

For me, walking in true forgiveness was a difficult process at first. But, by the grace of Father God which flowed like a continual stream within my marriage, I was able to completely forgive my husband as God had also forgiven me. I will add that a few of the main contributing factors which made it so difficult for me to initially forgive God's way occurred because I had allowed my flesh to respond negatively with what happened in my marriage.

At the very beginning when I petitioned God concerning the direction He wanted me to take for my marriage, I did not completely follow through with His full instructions. The second thing that contributed to my long process of learning how to walk in true forgiveness towards my husband was the fact that I responded to him with love that had been bruised and defiled by the cares of life. Instead of responding to him in love as Father God does when we have fallen short, I responded in bitterness of heart. That's why it's so important to allow yourself to first go through the process of emotional healing God's way, because your responses will dictate how well the reconciliation process will flow within your marriage.

Step Two: Questions for Self-Reflection

1. What other issues have you faced within your marriage? Explain

2. Was your spouse's affair the only breach to your marriage covenant? Explain

3. Have you always been faithful in your marriage? Explain

4. Have you had issues with walking in forgiveness in the past? Explain

5. Have you forgiven your spouse? Explain

6. Have you forgiven the person/people involved in your spouse's affair/affairs?

7. Have you forgiven yourself? Explain

8. Have you forgiven and released God for any ill feelings you may have against Him? Explain

9. Are you praying for yourself? Explain

10. Are you praying for your spouse? Explain

11. Have you prayed for the person/people involved in your spouse's affair/affairs? Explain

Proverbs 3:5-6
Trust in the Lord with all of your heart and lean not unto your own understanding; in all your ways acknowledge Him and He shall direct your paths.

Step Three: Renewing Covenant Trust (Mind)

Free your mind and your body will follow

"I look to the hills from which comes my help. Knowing the heavenly Father is the only one who reaches way down to heal all of the pain that I have felt. I look for the strength to try to trust you again. I know it will not be easy as my heart is truly on the mend. Because of the great love that Father God has shown to me, I will honor the God that I see in you and allow for our new season of trust to begin."

Thus far, we have discussed how to assess your wounds (heart) and how to walk in forgiveness (spirit) with your spouse. The next step of emotional healing God's way is learning how to renew your covenant trust (mind). This is a very important step because without the ability to renew trust, all of the other areas in your marriage which need trust to stand upon would eventually fail.

Trust is described as: **Firm reliance on the integrity, ability, or character of a person or thing.**

Having trust and walking in a place of security is extremely important not only in a covenant marriage but in all relationships. Without trust, which serves as the glue which holds everything together, many relationships get stuck in the developmental stages.

How do you learn to freely trust again, especially after betrayal? How can you regain the trust you and your spouse once shared? No matter what you may eventually decide concerning the future direction of your marriage, learning how to trust again is not only for your spouse's benefit but for yours as well.

Below are three steps which will help assist you as you begin the process of renewing covenant trust with your spouse:

1. Humble yourself and allow God the opportunity to transform your way of thinking.

Humbling yourself will allow for God to meet you right where you are. Many times when a person has experienced hurt or pain, they immediately move into the role of a victim. When this happens, self -preservation is the person's only concern. By allowing God the opportunity to transform your thinking, your focus shifts from that of victim to victor and survivor.

2. Allow the light of the Holy Spirit to reveal the broken areas of trust from your past.

One of the roles of the Holy Spirit is that of a comforter. When the comforter comes, healing can take place in the deep broken areas of trust in your life. Whether the places of broken trust have lain dormant for many years, now is the time to allow the light of God's presence to reveal those broken areas so covenant trust can be restored.

3. Release your spouse from the emotional prison you may have placed them in.

Unlock your spouse's cell to allow them the room to grow and renew covenant trust according to God's plan for their lives. Don't try to dictate or control the process that they may need to go through. This is especially important since your spouse – as the entry point of the breech in your covenant relationship – may need additional time to walk through the grief process.

As you allow God the opportunity to flow and move as He desires in your life, you will begin to realize that not only have you matured during the emotional healing process but you may have healed at a pace quicker than what you anticipated on the front end.

Learning to trust again in a Christ-like manner may seem hard at first. But, as you learn and embrace God's way for healing, you will see that it is healthier and a lot less stressful than trying to heal in a worldly manner where revenge is the order of the day.

When your ability to trust aligns itself with God's purpose and plan for your life, you can be assured that the divine wisdom He releases will add value that will carry you for the rest of your life. As you renew covenant trust first with God and then yourself, learning to trust your spouse in a godly manner will strengthen the foundation of your marriage covenant like never before.

As you prepare to answer the self-reflection questions for this chapter, take a few moments to think on the goodness of God in your life. If you reflect on the path you have traveled since you were born, you will realize that the forgiveness of God has been sprinkled throughout your life's tapestry.

Personal Testimony Nugget

Renewing covenant trust in my marriage went hand-in-hand with forgiving my husband and myself. Because I initially walked in anger and unforgiveness with him, it was hard for me to trust my husband at first. But later in 2003 when I also committed adultery, it was then that I had the true understanding of what God had been saying to me all along as He walked me though the book of Hosea in the Bible.

Hardening my heart towards my husband and not being open nor willing to trust him actually opened a door in my life for the enemy to come right in as I too also fell to the same temptation. The whole event surrounding my fall humbled me to the core because I was now in the place of having to go to my husband to seek forgiveness for the very same sin that he committed. It is important to remember that God trusts us with our bodies, family, gifts and possessions daily. How much more should we be ready and willing to forgive, release and renew covenant trust with our spouse? After all, forgiveness is the main reason that we are all here today. If it wasn't for God's forgiveness, where would we be?

Step Three: Questions for Self-Reflection

1. Have you received Christ as your Lord and Savior? Explain

2. At what point did you receive your salvation? Before, during or after your marriage? Explain

3. Is your spouse saved?

4. List some of your strengths? Explain

5. List some of your weaknesses? Explain

6. Do you speak positively or negatively to others concerning your spouse? Explain

7. Have you had issues with trust in the past? Explain

8. Where would you like to see yourself spiritually in the next five years? Explain

9. Now that you have embarked on the pathway to healing, are you willing to share this information with others who may need the same encouragement?

10. Are you willing to trust God and walk in obedience to what He reveals concerning your marriage? Explain

Song of Solomon 7:10
I am my beloveds and his desire is toward me.

Song of Solomon 8:10
I am a wall and my breasts like towers; then I became in his eyes as one who found peace.

Step Four: Reclaiming Covenant Intimacy (Body)

You, Me & God. Just the three of us.

"Intimacy means you, me and nobody else but God at the center of our relationship. Know that I have forgiven and released you from submitting to the sins of your flesh. I forgive you for giving your body to someone outside of our covenant bond. Although completely forgiven, I must ask for you to please be patient and allow time for me to get back into the groove of our covenant marriage flow."

We have reached the final step in the process which leads to embracing total emotional healing God's way. The journey and path leading up to this final step may have been difficult for some more than others. As mentioned earlier, the divine purpose for this book was to help guide you as an individual along the pathway to finding peace and freedom in every area of your life. My prayer is that you are now standing in the peace of God which I experienced at this point. Truth be told, if you were to remain in the same broken state as you did when you first knew of your spouse's affair, your heart would have become calloused to the healing and hope that God destined for you to experience.

Before we move forward with the subject of reclaiming covenant intimacy, let's take a moment to look back over the three previous steps.

Starting with the area of the heart, you were shown how to begin the healing process by pressing pause so you could assess your wounds. The next step, which represented the spirit, focused on you walking in true forgiveness. The third step involved the body and revealed steps on how you could renew covenant trust with your spouse.

The last step to emotional healing God's way calls for reclaiming covenant intimacy. So what exactly does the word *intimacy* mean?

It can be described as: **Marked by close acquaintance, association or familiarity.**

In covenant marriage, it is extremely important to know and understand what intimacy is because not everything in marriage is about sexual intercourse. Rather, the focus should be more on the relationship itself. Having great covenant intimacy with your spouse did not begin when you met but actually begin in your relationship with the Heavenly Father. As you draw near to God to become one in fellowship with Him, the result is your spouse receiving the overflow of love and intimacy that you have in your heart for the Father.

As you minister to (love, serve and assist) your spouse, the Father will be pleased because your acts of service towards your spouse are a representation of your relationship with the Father.

So how do you begin to reclaim covenant intimacy after an affair? Listed below are some healthy ways to help assist you as you begin the process:

1. If you have not already done so, make a visit to your nearest clinic or health care professional to get tested for HIV/AIDS and any other STD's (sexually transmitted disease).

2. Maintain a place of peace mentally. Never allow yourself to become so consumed with the cares of life that your peace is lost in the process.

3. Be sensitive concerning your expectations for your spouse. Be realistic and don't allow images from some of the current reality shows to serve as the foundation for how your covenant marriage should operate. Always use the word of God and His wisdom as your guide.

4. Set aside time daily for fellowship with God. Spending time alone in His presence will help aid you in reconnecting with your spouse.

5. Spend time in prayer and intercession for your marriage. Make it a point to invite God into your marriage relationship on a daily basis.

6. Work to help make your home a haven of rest and peace. Make a special effort to filter out all negative outside influences.

7. Ensure that you and your spouse have a weekly date night. Use this time to reconnect outside the home with each other.

Although this is not a complete list of all of the things which you can do to reclaim covenant intimacy in your marriage, it does however provide you with some strategic things to do in order to begin the process of moving forward. My prayer for you as you begin or continue in your process of drawing close the Father, is that your marriage relationship receives the necessary jump start that's needed to increase intimacy in your union.

As you close out this final chapter, take a few moments to press pause before answering the self-reflection questions. Allow yourself the opportunity to reflect upon the journey you have traveled since picking up this book. Celebrate and give God the glory for your healing and deliverance. Thank Him for guiding you through this process. And, remember to allow all the pain you've experienced in your covenant marriage to make you a better – and not a bitter – spouse.

Personal Testimony Nugget

Before my husband and I were able to get back to a place to reclaiming our covenant intimacy, God directed me to an extended period of consecration. Because we both had defiled our marriage bed and broken covenant earlier in our marriage, it was imperative that I needed to go through the cleansing process as orchestrated by the Father. The first step was repentance and the process of being restored back to intimacy and fellowship with God. After this, my husband and I went through a period where we actually dated like we did before we were married. It was a year-long process (from 2004 through 2005) which was not only necessary but also served as a blessing because the foundation which was shaken had an opportunity to be reinforced in the places where there was structural weakness.

While I walked through my process to reclaiming covenant

intimacy, God reminded me that the process was similar to what He goes through with His children. When both my husband and I broke covenant, it blocked fellowship with the Father. But after a time of repentance, the relationship was restored as God accepted us back with open arms and into covenant fellowship with Him.

Step Four: Questions for Self-Reflection

1. At this stage in the healing process, how do you feel emotionally and physically? Explain

2. Now that you have completed this self-help book, what are your thoughts concerning your marriage now? Explain

3. Are you able to look your spouse in the eye without having any resentment in your heart? Explain

4. Have you reconnected with your spouse intimately since the ending of their affair? Explain

5. If you and your spouse are separated or seeking to divorce since you have read this book, what do you hear God speaking to you concerning your next step? Explain

6. How do you view your relationship with God? Has your relationship changed with Him since you read this book? Explain

7. Now that you are well on the pathway to healing, are you willing to embrace the total process to grow deeper in your relationship with God? Explain

Prayer of Thanks

Heavenly Father,

I come before you today to give you honor, glory and praise. I lift your name on high as I speak forth into the atmosphere that you are a great and a good God. There is no one anywhere who can do me the way that you do. There is no one who takes care of me like you do. There is no one who loves me like you do. There is no one who provides for me like you do.

I give you praise and honor for your faithfulness towards me. I thank you for watching over my life and covering me with your mercy. You are the great I AM, and you are sovereign and holy. Thank you for where you have brought me from. Thank you for bringing me through the hurt, pain, rejection and shame.

Thank you for allowing your healing to flow in my life. Thank you for your peace. Thank you for keeping my mind. Thank you for healing my heart. Thank you for restoring my soul. Thank you for making me whole again.

Thank you for where you are taking me even now. I say thank you, thank you, thank you, Father. Thank you for setting me free. In Jesus name, I give you glory. Amen.

Prayer for Forgiveness

Heavenly Father,

I humble myself under your mighty hand. I thank you for this opportunity to bring glory, honor and praise to your name. First, I ask that you create in me a clean heart and renew a right spirit within me. I ask for your forgiveness for allowing any anger, hatred or bitterness to reside in my heart for far too long.

Father, I seek forgiveness for using my spouse's affair as an excuse to manipulate, harm or to retaliate against them. Forgive me for turning my back on my spouse and for shutting down the pathway to real communication between us.

I freely forgive and I freely release my spouse for their participation in the affair. I freely forgive and freely release the person or persons with whom my spouse defiled our marriage bed. I realize now that they may or may not have known my spouse was married. Regardless of whether they participated of their own free will or unknowingly, I release them now into your capable hands and ask that you heal them in every area of their lives as well.

I bind up all hurt and pain, and release myself from the betrayal, rejection and shame associated with this affair. I break off all curses, fear, and low self-esteem associated with adultery. I now loose your love, peace, joy and acceptance in my life. And, I proclaim that I am victorious and no longer a victim. I thank you Father that now I walk in total healing and freedom because Jesus Christ has already come and set me free. Amen.

Prayer for Wisdom and Direction

Heavenly Father,

I come before you to thank you for my life and give you glory. Thank you for your goodness shown toward me. Thank you for being my strength during the time of testing. Thank you for covering me under the shadow of your wings. I give you praise just for being the wonderful God that you are.

Today, I seek you for your divine wisdom and direction. I ask that you lead and guide me into your perfect will and way. I decrease and humble myself that you may increase in my life. Order my steps according to your established holy word.

I die to my own way and to any impure motives, and I freely accept your divine purpose for my life. Today, I ask that you take my life and use it for your honor and your glory. In Jesus name, I pray. Amen.

Prophetic Prayer for Marriages

Dear Heavenly Father,

I lift up all covenant marriages before you this day. Where emotional or physical affairs have occurred, I bind up all residue of betrayal, hurt, pain, rejection and shame in the name of Jesus. I break and destroy in the realm of the spirit the power of the enemy over each and every marriage you have ordained. I decree and declare that the anointing and healing salve of the Sovereign Father is now filling the hearts and the minds of these covenant couples.

Father, I thank you for those who have purchased this book to gain wisdom, insight and understanding on how to heal emotionally as you desire. May their cup be filled until it overflows into their marriage relationship.

Thank you Father for opening up each couple's eyes and ears to see and to hear what you have to say to their hearts. I thank you that they will no longer allow their emotions to take control and lead them astray and into bondage. I thank you that the fruit of the spirit is made evident in their lives on a daily basis. I thank you that these covenant marriages are a true representation of Christ and His bride (the church).

I decree and declare that these covenant couples will walk in spiritual wholeness, spirit, soul and body. I decree and declare that your divine order is established in every area of their lives. Thank you Father for a heightened hedge of protection over each marriage. Thank you for the precious blood of Jesus covering their lives, home and all you have allowed them to be steward over.

I decree and declare that the Godly deposit sown into their lives on this day will take root and bring forth fruit and a multiplied spiritual harvest at its appointed time. I stand to rejoice with these covenant couples as they accept and receive an outpouring of your love, grace, joy and peace. In Jesus name. Amen.

Prayer of Salvation

If after reading this book you have a desire to know Jesus as your personal Lord and Savior, please pray the following prayer:

Heavenly Father,

I repent of all of my sins and right now, I do confess that Jesus is the Son of God and that He died for the remission of my sins.

I believe that Jesus died and was buried and rose again, and is now seated at the right hand of God in Heaven.

I receive Him now as Lord of my life and I now commit to serve him for the rest of my days.

It's in Jesus' name I pray. Amen.

If you have just prayed this prayer and want more information about beginning your new life as a Christian, please write or email us at the following and we will be happy to send you a free booklet:

Unity Three Publications
PO BOX 754301
Memphis, TN 38175
arnitafields@yahoo.com

Spiritual & Counseling Resources

After the Affair: Emotional Healing God's Way
Counseling Sessions for Individuals, Couples and
Support Groups
P. O. Box 754301
Memphis, Tennessee 38175
aftertheaffairseminars@yahoo.com

American Association of Christian Counselors
www.aacc.net/resources/find-a-counselor

Emotional Fitness Centers of Tennessee
The Healing Center
3885 Tchulahoma Road
Memphis, TN 38118
www.memphishealingcenter.com
(901) 370-HOPE (4673)

Life Change Counseling Center
4092 Lace Wood Dr.
Memphis, TN 38115
www.n2newdirection.org
(901) 334-5378

My Therapist - Online Resource
www.mytherapist.com

National Institute of Mental Health
www.nimh.nih.gov

Prepare - Enrich Program
The Online Couple Checkup
www.prepare-enrich.com

About the Author

Birthed forth into the Kingdom of God and set apart as a modern day Scribe, Arnita L. Fields has authored nine books and several collections of poetry. As a prophetic writer, she pens prophetic words, blog posts and articles which help to edify, encourage and instruct the Body of Christ on how to walk in the divine truth of the Heavenly Father. The books she has been blessed to author include, *Rescued, Restored, Renewed and Revived a Collection of Christian Poems, (2006) And the Beat Goes On, Poems from a Restored Marriage (2007), The Word a Poetry Connection (2008), America's Change a Poetic View (2009)* and *Drop that Bottle, and Pick up a Fork! (2011)*. Arnita also served as co-author of two faith-filled anthologies: *This Far by Faith (2008)* and *Keeping the Faith (2011)*.

Her first self-help book, *Covenant Sisterhood: Embracing Heaven's Divine Connections (2011)* – which was written to help transform relationships among women – was released to great reviews. Shortly following its official release, the book became the official membership book for two national women's ministries. Featured over the last few years as a guest on several online radio programs, Arnita has shared with listeners her journey as an author and passionate advocate for healthy covenant marriages.

In addition to being an award-winning author, Arnita is a graduate of Liberty University with a degree in Psychology & Christian Counseling. She holds additional certifications in biblical, pre-marital and marriage counseling.

If you would like to contact Arnita, send an email to arnitafields@yahoo.com or visit her blog at arnitalfields.blogspot.com.